Japke Karreman

Cruise tourism development in a small destination

Japke Karreman

Cruise tourism development in a small destination

LAP LAMBERT Academic Publishing

Impressum / Imprint

Bibliografische Information der Deutschen Nationalbibliothek: Die Deutsche Nationalbibliothek verzeichnet diese Publikation in der Deutschen Nationalbibliografie; detaillierte bibliografische Daten sind im Internet über http://dnb.d-nb.de abrufbar.

Alle in diesem Buch genannten Marken und Produktnamen unterliegen warenzeichen-, marken- oder patentrechtlichem Schutz bzw. sind Warenzeichen oder eingetragene Warenzeichen der jeweiligen Inhaber. Die Wiedergabe von Marken, Produktnamen, Gebrauchsnamen, Handelsnamen, Warenbezeichnungen u.s.w. in diesem Werk berechtigt auch ohne besondere Kennzeichnung nicht zu der Annahme, dass solche Namen im Sinne der Warenzeichen- und Markenschutzgesetzgebung als frei zu betrachten wären und daher von jedermann benutzt werden dürften.

Bibliographic information published by the Deutsche Nationalbibliothek: The Deutsche Nationalbibliothek lists this publication in the Deutsche Nationalbibliografie; detailed bibliographic data are available in the Internet at http://dnb.d-nb.de.

Any brand names and product names mentioned in this book are subject to trademark, brand or patent protection and are trademarks or registered trademarks of their respective holders. The use of brand names, product names, common names, trade names, product descriptions etc. even without a particular marking in this works is in no way to be construed to mean that such names may be regarded as unrestricted in respect of trademark and brand protection legislation and could thus be used by anyone.

Coverbild / Cover image: www.ingimage.com

Verlag / Publisher:
LAP LAMBERT Academic Publishing
ist ein Imprint der / is a trademark of
AV Akademikerverlag GmbH & Co. KG
Heinrich-Böcking-Str. 6-8, 66121 Saarbrücken, Deutschland / Germany
Email: info@lap-publishing.com

Herstellung: siehe letzte Seite /
Printed at: see last page
ISBN: 978-3-659-42079-5

Table of contents

1. Introduction

1.1 Cruise tourism

In the past two decades, Tourism has grown by 300 percent and with a growth rate of 5.9 percent it is one of the fastest growing industries globally. It is the second largest industry in the world. For some countries, it is the most important source of revenue. Tourism also generates many jobs, more than 74 million worldwide in 2003. It generates 3.8 percent of global GDP (Bailey *et al.* 2004).

Already more than 100 years ago, a form of cruise tourism existed, but modern cruise tourism originated in the early 1970s in Miami, US. It started with cruises throughout the Caribbean and then developed into a worldwide industry (World Tourism Organization 2010). It is one of the fastest growing tourism industries (Cruise Norway 2011). In the first few decades after its emergence, the cruise industry had a growth rate of more than 8 percent. Up to 2020 a growth rate of 4.1 percent has been forecasted (Bailey *et al.* 2004; World Tourism Organization 2010).

In 2003, 9.8 million people took a holiday on a cruise ship. This generated 14.7 billion US dollar in gross revenues. This was 3.2 percent more than the previous year. The cruise line industry is dominated by North America, which accounts for 80 percent of cruise ship passengers. In 2003, 7.9 million cruise tourists started their cruise in North America. The Caribbean is the most popular destination, followed by the Mediterranean and Europe (Bailey *et al.* 2004).

The cruise industry can sustain high growth rates due to the continuous investments in innovation and improvement. New ships are built every year, with higher capacity and innovative facilities and activities. Also the marketing is handled in an innovative way (World Tourism Organization 2010).

In the whole of Europe the cruise industry created 307,526 jobs in 2010, which created a total income of €9.3 billion. For small destinations this means mostly some jobs in transport and utilities and hospitality, which together account for 18 percent of the total employment and 20 percent of the total income (G.P. Wild (International) Limited & Business Research & Economic Advisors 2011).

1.2 Cruise tourism in Norway

According to a survey conducted in 2010, the cruise tourism sector in Norway creates around 1,600 jobs in the high season and 1,100 jobs outside the season. The economic impact is approximately 2 billion kroner per year, which is around 260 million Euros. When indirect effects are included, cruise tourism is estimated to create 3,200 jobs in the high season and 2,200 jobs outside the season. The economic impact is then 4 billion kroner, which is around 520 million Euros. The employment effects are the highest in small ports (Handelsdepartementet 2012).

The total amount of cruise passengers coming to Norway has almost doubled from 1.1 million in 2006 to more than 2 million in 2011. Even though less ships come to Norway, the amount of passengers increases, because the ships are getting bigger (Cruise Norway 2011). In 2011 Norway had 41 cruise ports, of which 30 were active. In the same year 13 of those had more than 50 calls. The biggest markets for Norway are the UK and Germany, followed by the US, Italy, Spain, France and the Netherlands (NHO Reiseliv 2010).

In 2001 there came 195 cruise ship to Bergen. From these ships, 104,766 passengers came on land, who spend a total of 63 million kroner. In Hardanger there came 39 ships, divided over Eidfjord, Jondal and Ulvik. Those three places got respectively 19, 3 and 17 ships. A total of 17,500 passengers came on land, which all together spend 5.8 million kroner, of which 4.5 million kroner for tours and shopping. That is an average of 331 kroner per passenger. In Bergen the average spending of passengers was 600 kroner and crew spend around 300 kroner per person. People spend more in Bergen than in Hardanger, because there are more shopping opportunities in Bergen (Andersen & Ellingsen 2003).

1.3 Study site

Skjolden lies innermost in the Sognefjord, the longest navigable fjord in the world. The closest large town is Sogndal and is one and a half hour away by car. There are some other small towns around Skjolden, like Gaupne and Hafslo. Skjolden can be reached via Sogndal and in summer also via the Sognefjellet. Approximately 300 people live in Skjolden (Cruise Destination Skjolden - Sognefjord 2012).

Although Skjolden already received some form of cruise tourism more than 100 years ago, the first modern cruise ships came to Skjolden in 2008. In 2008 and 2009 there was not yet a cruise quay in Skjolden, so the ships would anchor and tender boats were used to ship passengers to the land. Those two years were used as try outs to see whether cruise tourism in Skjolden was desirable and possible. In 2008 there came 5 cruise ships and in 2009 there came 13. In 2010 a cruise quay was build, and there came 11 cruise ships. In 2011 the cruise quay was officially opened and again 11 ships called in Skjolden. In 2012 there came 21 cruise ships to Skjolden, with a total number of passengers of 30,000 (Cruise Norway 2011).

The quay has a length of about 130 metres, and can therefore accommodate all current sizes of ships and is prepared for even bigger ships. At the quay there is a service building with a restaurant and from 2012 also a souvenir shop. The distance to the centre of Skjolden is approximately 700 metres (Cruise Destination Skjolden - Sognefjord 2012).

Choice of study area

I choose Skjolden as a case for this study, because it is a small destination and it only recently got cruise tourism. It is important to see how things can be done sustainable from an early stage in the development. I also took some interviews in Olden and Flåm, to get a better understanding. Olden and Flåm have a much longer history of cruise tourism.

1.4 Main objective and research questions

The main objective of this thesis is to gain insight into how a small destination can develop cruise tourism in a sustainable way.

Explanation of objective

Tourism is one of the fastest growing industries in the world and cruise tourism is one of the biggest growing sub-industries of tourism. It is important that destinations maintain some control over the development of cruise tourism (and tourism in general), so they are not impacted in a negative way. In order to learn more about this, a number of research questions become important:

How can **a small destination** develop cruise tourism in a sustainable way? The study is limited to small destinations. Development in small destinations is different than in big destinations, for example because the impacts are

6

different. If 3000 people visit a town of 300 residents, the impact is much bigger than if they visit a city with several hundred thousand inhabitants.

How can a small destination **develop** cruise **tourism** in a sustainable way?
It is important to know about tourism development in general, to know what factors are important.
This resulted in the first research question:
Q1: What factors are important for the development of (cruise) tourism of a (small) destination?
This question in answered by describing destination development in general.

How can a small destination develop **cruise tourism** in a sustainable way?
Then it is important to know the differences between land based tourism and cruise tourism.

How can a small destination develop cruise tourism **in a sustainable way**?
Sustainability in this case is meant as both economic, socio-cultural and environmental sustainability. It is important that the development of cruise tourism brings more positive than negative impacts. The managers of a destination should know the impacts and know to what extend those impacts can be influenced.
This resulted in two more research questions:
Q2: What are the impacts of cruise tourism on a small destination?
This question is answered by using the literature of what impacts are known to be related to tourism and cruise tourism.
Q3: What are the attitudes of the residents about cruise tourism in a small destination?
Different people react different to certain impacts. Some impacts are negative to one person and positive to another person.

1.5 Overview

In chapter 1 I describe the background of cruise tourism development in general and in Norway. I describe the study area, Skjolden. Also I present my main question along with three research questions.

Chapter 2, the theory, is divided in three parts, based on the research questions. Part 2.1 is based on the first research question: What factors are important for the development of (cruise) tourism of a (small) destination? It describes why people go on a certain holiday, the so called push factors, and what people base their choice of destination on, the so called pull factors. Then it discusses the different stages in tourism development, which is important to know about if one want to have an influence on the development. Finally this part talks about important differences between land based tourism and cruise tourism, in term of transport, service, food, accommodation and the organisation of the industry. Part 2.2 is based on the research question: What are the impacts of cruise tourism on a small destination? The impacts are divided into economic, socio-cultural and environmental impacts. Both positive and negative impacts are described. Part 2.3 looks at the research question: What are the attitudes of the residents about cruise tourism in a small destination? It looks at what is being said in the literature about residents attitudes to tourism. Also it looks at some articles which describe the attitudes of residents in some case studies, one of which is related to cruise tourism.

Chapter 3 describes the methods that I used and the execution of them.

In chapter 4 I describe the results of the interviews. Sometimes I use quotes of a respondent, but mostly I summarise and interpret what the respondents said. The results are divided into the same three parts as the theory, and those parts thus relate to the three research questions. The information from the interviews is also compared to the relevant theories about it. On top of the three parts relating to the research questions, the results start with a part about the role of Røysi, Luster municipality and the cruise companies on the development of cruise tourism in Skjolden.

Chapter 5 gives a critical look at the paper and looks at the reliability and the validity.

Chapter 6 is the conclusion.

2. Theory

2.1 Tourism development

2.1.1 Push and pull factors

Tourism has been growing rapidly and is now one of the biggest industries in the world. The factors that stimulate the demand for tourism can be called push factors. Below are some important push factors (Weaver & Lawton 2010):

• Economic factors

When countries get richer, the people, or at least the ones with more money, can travel more.

• Social factors

During the years, people have gotten more free time, and thus travelling has become a bigger part of life. Also the attitude to tourism has changed.

• Demographic factors

Reduced family size, population increase, urbanisation and increased life expectancy are all factors that contribute in a growth in tourism.

• Technological factors

Improving transportation systems and information technology, e.g. computerised reservation systems, make the tourism industry more accessible.

• Political factors

Certain political factors, such as more open borders, lessen the restriction to travel, so more people can and will travel.

A destination cannot easily influence push factors, but it can influence pull factors. There are many different pull factors. It depends on the destination which are the most important pull factors (Weaver & Lawton 2010):

• Geographical proximity to markets

More tourists come from close by than from far away, because the cost of travelling to the destination. To compensate this, destinations can increase the marketing in far away origin regions.

- Accessibility to markets

Better infrastructural and political accessibility will attract more tourists.

- Availability of attractions

Attractions differ in terms of quality, quantity, diversity, uniqueness, carrying capacity, market image and accessibility. There are pre-existing and created attractions, the latter of which could be built attractions, but could for example also be festivals. Attractions can be susceptible to fashion or change in demand.

- Cultural links

Tourists might prefer to go to countries more similar to their own, based on culture, language and/or religion.

- Availability of services

It is important for a destination to provide proper services, such as accommodation, toilets and dining facilities.

- Affordability

Exchange rates of a country cannot be influenced by destination managers, but if the high prices are a problem, they could do more marketing for higher-end markets.

- Peace, stability and safety

A destination is more attracting if it is save to go there, when there is no war and less crime and terrorism. Destinations are also more attracting if there are less natural disasters, if the drinking water and the food are safe, if there are less diseases and if the traffic is safer.

- Positive market image

The market image is based on many of the above factors. It can be descriptive, the objective perception, or evaluative, the subjective perception. Marketing can be important in creating a positive market image.

- Pro-tourism policies

Policies can be implemented to increase the pull factor of a destination. One example is a campaign amongst the residents to promote a welcoming attitude towards the tourists.

2.1.2 Different stages in tourism development

The most common way to describe the development of a tourist destination is by use of Butlers destination cycle, also called the Butler sequence (Butler 1980; Weaver & Lawton 2010). This is a model describing five stages of growth, which are exploration, involvement, development, consolidation and stagnation. A prerequisite for the use of this model is that there is a free market and the demand conditions are sustained. The five stages of the model can be followed by continued stagnation, decline or rejuvenation, depending on how the destination manager responds to them (Butler 1980; Weaver & Lawton 2010).

During the exploration stage, only a small number of visitors come to a destination. It is very new for the residents of the destination, and they are still curious. The visitors are welcome and may even be allowed to sit in on cultural traditions and sleep in residents' houses. The residents are still very much in control due to the small number of visitors, so the relationship with the visitors is good. The visitors use local services, for example they buy their food on the local market and use the local bus system for getting around. Therefore the local economy benefits from the visitors, though the total economic impact is not yet very large (Butler 1980; Weaver & Lawton 2010).

When more visitors come, a destination goes into the involvement stage. This is characterised by the emergence of small guest houses, eating places, small guiding companies and semi-commercial attractions. It can still be as simple as residents making available some rooms in their house for a small fee. Due to the provision of such services, the amount of visitors will increase. Residents are still positive and welcoming, because there are not so many visitors that they have a negative impact on the social and natural environment, but there are enough visitors for the locals to earn some money on them. As the involvement stage goes along, the tourism becomes more commercial and official and impacts increase. The residents have to find ways to cope with the increasing tourism. One way to cope is the implementation, consciously or subconsciously, of frontstage and backstage places or activities. An example of this is that tourists are not allowed to sit in on cultural traditions, but the residents may perform such cultural traditions in a somewhat altered way to the tourists and possibly ask an entrance fee for this (Butler 1980; Weaver & Lawton 2010).

The development stage consists of a rapid growth of the tourism industry and big changes in a small amount of time. How fast and in what way this growth occurs, depends on the pull factors of a destination and on how the development is attempted to be managed. Due to the rapid change, the destination loses some of it control, which is taken over by non-local companies. The landscape changes, as small guest houses are being replaced by large hotels and agricultural land makes way for golf courses. The uniqueness associated with the destination during the exploration and involvement stage disappears. The negative impact on the environment increases quickly. Tourists are not new and exciting anymore for the residents, and as the number of tourists increases, the attitude of the residents towards them becomes more negative (Butler 1980; Weaver & Lawton 2010).

During the consolidation stage the growth rate of tourism in a destination decreases, while the total amount does still increase. Usually the number of tourists over a year is more than the total number of residents. Carrying capacities, both environmental, social and economic, are being exceeded. The economy of a destination is dominated by tourism, and therefore becomes highly seasonal. Authentic natural and cultural attractions are being replaced by commercial attractions, such as theme parks. Some residents become antagonistic towards tourists, while others resign themselves to the situation and adjust to it or leave the area (Butler 1980; Weaver & Lawton 2010).

During the stagnation stage the amount of tourism exceeds the capacity of the destination, which leads to price wars and deterioration of the products and services. The destination becomes less desirable and less new tourists come to visit (Butler 1980; Weaver & Lawton 2010).

The stagnation stage can continue to exist over a long period of time, but usually it evolves into either decline or rejuvenation. Decline is characterised by failing efforts to attract new tourists, lack or failed attempts to revitalise tourism in the destination and possibly tourists stay away due to a negative image of the destination because of negativity of the residents. Also tourism may decrease because there are more interesting tourism destinations elsewhere, which are a better alternative for the tourists. Tourist services are abandoned and hotels are converted into other types of businesses. Tourism is no longer the main industry in the area. Rejuvenation is another stage that can follow stagnation, or it can come after decline. Rejuvenation is the changing of the tourism products in a destination or at least improving the image, so that a destination can once again have a blooming tourism industry. Rejuvenation is generally not something that happens by itself, it is a deliberate process, involving destination managers and entrepreneurs. Both the public and the private sector have an important role in the rejuvenation of a destination (Butler 1980; Weaver & Lawton 2010).

Changes from one stage to the next are usually a transition rather than a sharp boundary, although a specific event can speed up the process. Such events can be internal or external. An example of an internal event is the construction of the first large resort. External events can be for example word-of-mouth marketing or the visit of a celebrity. Such events are especially influential for the transition from the exploration to the involvement stage, because there the change has the most impact. Internal events are the most beneficial here, because then it is easiest for the destination to remain control over the development. A big external event can cause very rapid growth in tourism and not every destination can keep up with this. After only a short involvement stage, the destination will go on to the development stage (Weaver & Lawton 2010).

In order to sustainably develop a destination, it is important that destination managers are aware of those events or factors which trigger change in the destination cycle. They need to know which factors they can influence and what is the best reaction to the factors that they cannot control. Both internal and external factors can be divided into intentional and unintentional actions. Factors in each of those four dimensions can be stimulants or depressants. Internal-intentional factors are most desirable. Stimulants can be the improvement of infrastructure, marketing done by the destination and local investments in tourism. Depressants are for example entry fees or infrastructural restrictions in order to restrict tourism growth. The least desirable are the external-unintentional factors. Natural disasters can be a depressant for the destination that is directly affected by it, while it can be a stimulant for other destinations in the area, because they function as an alternative to the affected destination. Internal-unintentional factors are generally negative, like the destruction of a coral reef due to local pollution. External-intentional factors can be the result of devaluation in the country's currency, which is a depressant for the country itself, but can be a stimulant for the surrounding countries (Weaver & Lawton 2010).

Of course there is also critique to the Butler sequence. Part of tourism developments conformed to the model to a certain extent, and part deviated from it. The model can be seen as an ideal type, to which one can compare the real development. Also the model assumes that active management is needed to avoid the destruction that the development cycle automatically leads to (Weaver & Lawton 2010).

There have been proposed alternative scenarios to the Butler sequence, based on proactive management; the supply-driven scenario and the demand-driven scenario. The supply-driven scenario implies that the amount of tourists is regulated to keep it under the threshold for carrying capacity. This is characterised by inducing slow growth during a long involvement stage and then consolidation at a level that is desirable. The reduction in demand can be achieved by measures like higher entry fees for attractions or the whole region or by restricting the number of visitors allowed. The development stage is avoided. In the demand-driven scenario, the threshold for carrying capacity is being increased along with the increasing number of tourists, during normal progression of the involvement and development stage. There are several ways to increase the carrying capacity. Some examples are tourist and resident education and awareness programs, the improvement of facilities for sewage and water treatment and expanding the local industries so that more of the necessary products can be obtained from local sources (Weaver & Lawton 2010).

2.1.3 Differences between cruise tourism and land based tourism

Land-based tourism consists of four parts; activities, accommodation, food and transport (Kamfjord 2003). In cruise tourism all the different parts are taken together. The cruise ship transports the tourists to different harbours. The tourists sleep on the ship and most of the time also eat on the ship. Also there are a lot of different activities organised on board. When the ship is in a harbour, there is some land-based activity. The passengers can go on land by themselves and join activities, go somewhere to eat and they may use local transportation to get around. Most passengers choose to join an organised trip, which includes activities and/or sightseeing, use of transport and it can include food, usually lunch.

This has a consequence on who earns money on cruise tourism. For land based tourism, the individual suppliers of tourism services earn money, like the hotel and the attraction that people visit. Cruise companies get most of the money from cruise tourists, but also carry most of the costs. When the cruise tourist goes on land, income opportunities are generated for several people, depending on who does what.

2.2 Impacts of tourism development

Many studies have been done about the economic benefits of tourism, but it is also important to look at the negative economic effects, as well as socio-cultural and environmental effects. It is also important to realise that an effect that is positive to some, can be negative to others. Research has shown that overall the economic effects are mostly positive, the socio-cultural effects are mostly undesirable, and the environmental effects are mixed (Mathieson & Wall 1990). Below is an overview of the economic, socio-cultural and environmental effect that tourism can have on a destination.

2.2.1 Economic impact

Initially one of the most important impacts of tourism is the economic impact. There has especially been a lot of focus on the positive impacts, like generation of income, creation of job opportunities and improvement of infrastructure. Those positive impacts are important reasons why tourism exist in many destinations (Weaver & Lawton 2010). However, it is important to know whether the economic impacts are just positive. Also, even if the economic impacts would only be positive, it is important to set them against the socio-cultural and environmental impacts, which tend to be more negative. Below is a description of the mainly positive impacts of tourism. However, these positive impacts also have some negative sides which are described along with the positive impacts. Afterwards the mainly negative impacts are described in more detail.

Revenue

Tourism generates money. The important thing to look at here is how much of this money actually benefits the destination and how much flows out of the destination by means of leakage. Also one should look at how much money goes into it, in order to generate the income (Weaver & Lawton 2010).

Revenue can be divided into direct and indirect revenue. Direct revenue are all the expenses for goods and services paid by tourists. Part of this is expenses made in advance, for example paying for the tour package to the tourism agent at home. The other part is the money that is spend in the destination itself. Only part of what a tourists pays for a package tour benefits the destination, and only this part can be used for calculating the revenue for the destination. Another direct revenue comes from taxation (Weaver & Lawton 2010).

Direct revenue can be increased in different ways. It can be increased by expanding the number of visitors, by increasing the average length of stay of visitors and by increasing the average daily expenditure of the visitors (Weaver & Lawton 2010). Most cruise ships only stay in port during one day and not overnight. Therefore it is more feasible to increase direct revenue by receiving more visitors or making them spend more per visit.

The circulation of the direct expenditures in a destination forms the indirect revenue. This ongoing circulation is known as the multiplier effect. For example, someone in a destination has animals. He gets money from the tourists who look at his animals. Some of this money he uses to buy special fodder for the animals, which comes from outside the area, so this money leaks out of the area. Another part of the money he uses inside the destination to buy food for himself at the local store. The store holder uses some of this money to buy produce from outside the area, leakage, and some to buy things from within the area. As long as some of the money goes around in the area, it contributes to the multiplier effect. It is the respending of the money which originally was earned from tourism. Eventually all the money might leak out, but because of the multiplier effect, it was worth more to the destination than just the original amount (Mathieson & Wall 1990; Weaver & Lawton 2010).

The amount of leakage depends on what size area you look at. If you look at a small destination, the leakage will be higher than when you look at the whole region in which this destination lies. The destination might have to get produce from other places in the region, which means leakage out of the destination, but not out of the region (Mathieson & Wall 1990).

In Belize it is seen that not a lot of the revenue from cruise tourism actually benefits the economy of the destination. Most of the money goes to the cruise line companies and only some individuals in Belize. Around half of the income from tours and excursions which are bough on board goes to the cruise lines (Center on Ecotourism and Sustainable Development 2006). Since the cruise lines are from outside the destination, and sometimes also from another country, this money is leaked out of the destination and maybe even out of the country (Dwyer & Forsyth 1998).

Departure ports and the countries in which they lie also benefit from cruise tourism by visitors spending money to get to the departure port, and maybe spending a night in a hotel before the cruise commences. Tourists might combine the cruise with some touristic activity before or after the cruise, which they would not have done if they had not gone on the cruise. Ports visited along the way mostly earn money when visitors make direct expenditures, go on excursions, visit attractions, and go shopping. Ports also receive payments from operators, who have to pay charges for using a port and some other services (Dwyer & Forsyth 1998).

More money from land based tourists compared to cruise tourists
According to the Center on Ecotourism and Sustainable Development (2006) cruise tourists spend less money in a destination than land based tourists. Land based tourists spend on average US $50, while for cruise tourists this is only US $10. Data from the Belize Tourism Board (BTB) shows that even though 77.2% of all tourists in Belize are cruise tourists, they only account for 17.5% of all tourist expenditures (Center on Ecotourism and Sustainable Development 2006). Also despite their large number, the cruise tourists contribute less than 50% of tourist contributions for conservation of natural and archaeological destination sites (Center on Ecotourism and Sustainable Development 2006).

Job opportunities

Jobs are created, but they are highly seasonal. Also there are a lot of easy jobs, and only some management jobs. Often these are filled by people from outside the destination, causing more economic leakage. Also many of the easier jobs go to foreign seasonal workers, causing more leakage and less job opportunities for local residents (Weaver & Lawton 2010).

Apart from direct employment created from tourism, there is also indirect and induced employment created. Indirect employment can be the construction workers building a hotel or surgeons who sometimes operate on tourists (Weaver & Lawton 2010). Induced employment comes forth because those working in the tourist industry spend some of their money in the area, creating more work in other sectors. This contributes to the employment multiplier, in approximately the same way as with revenue (Mathieson & Wall 1990; Weaver & Lawton 2010).

Even though cruise tourists bring in less money per person, City tour guides in Belize say that cruise tourism guarantees work during certain days of the season, while land based tourism is more uncertain. It is also being said that more can be done to make more people benefit more from the revenue of cruise tourism in Belize (Center on Ecotourism and Sustainable Development 2006).

Entrepreneurial activity, economic structure and infrastructure

Apart from the direct effects of income and job creation, tourism can also have a positive effect on education, environmental awareness, conservation and infrastructure development. According to some, tourism contributes to the knowledge of and appreciation for natural and cultural sites and to the protection and conservation of such sites, as well as the creation of better infrastructures on the sites (Center on Ecotourism and Sustainable

Development 2006). Tourism can also contribute to the reduction of emigration from rural areas (Bailey *et al.* 2004).

The following economic impacts are generally seen as more negative:

Opportunity costs

If people use certain resources for tourism, those resources cannot be used for another industry. The cost of not being able to use the resources for another industry is called the opportunity cost. This does not have to be a negative impact. If the benefits from tourism are higher than from another industry and higher than the costs, then it is not negative (Mathieson & Wall 1990).

Overdependence on tourism

Even though the tourism industry is growing, it is also susceptible to changes, like price changes and fashion changes, as well as economic trends and political situations. Such changes are difficult to predict. To handle fluctuations in demand, destinations should not just depend on tourism and it is preferable to have diversity also within the tourism industry (Mathieson & Wall 1990).

Inflation and land values

Inflation due to tourism takes several forms. If tourism in a destination is expanding, more land is required to build hotels, attractions and other services for tourists. Because the demand for land increases, the land value goes up, so it gets also more expensive for all the locals living on the land. Another form of inflation occurs because the tourists may have more money to spend in the destination than the locals, either because the tourists are richer, or just because they are on holiday, so do not watch their spending so closely. The local shops may react by increasing their prices, which has negative effects for the local residents (Bailey *et al.* 2004; Mathieson & Wall 1990).

2.2.2 Social and cultural impacts

Social and cultural impacts can arise from several situations. Local residents can have encounters with tourists because they offer them a service, but also when they don't have a service to offer them. They might make use of the same beach or shop in the same store. There does not have to be direct contact between the residents and the tourists for impacts to occur. Just by seeing the tourists and witnessing their behaviour, local residents can be influenced by tourists (Mathieson & Wall 1990).

Socio-cultural impacts can be difficult to measure and they may differ from person to person. What is negative to one person, it not necessarily negative to someone else (Bailey *et al.* 2004). Several frameworks have been created to explain how residents react to tourism. The most well known is Doxey's irritation index, also called irridex (Weaver & Lawton 2010).

Tolerance of tourism depends on several factors. If host and tourists are culturally and economically more alike, then tolerance is more likely. The amount of tourists also has an effect on tolerance. An example of this is cruise tourism, where a large number of people arrive in a destination at the same time. Part of the cruise tourists might then go into the small city centre, possibly unaware or unprepared for the socio-cultural conditions in the destination area. Small destinations might have a lower tolerance than bigger destinations, because they have less capacity to absorb the tourists, which will thus be more obviously present. A slower development yields more tolerance than a very fast development, because then the local community has more time to adjust to the changes made by tourism (Mathieson & Wall 1990; Weaver & Lawton 2010).

In order for the local community to be more positive towards tourism development, it helps if they are involved in it. It is important that the local residents benefit from the tourism. One has to look at the long term as well as the short term, make sure the community and environment can keep up with the development and the infrastructure is developed enough. Also the focus should not be on tourism as the only source of revenue (Bailey et al. 2004).

It would be useful to educate tourists about the local culture and tradition (Bailey et al. 2004), especially if it is very different from what they are used to. If the tourists learn more about it, they will appreciate it more, and care more about the preservation of it.

Examples of social and cultural impacts can be changes in value systems, individual behaviour, family relationships, collective traditional life styles, safety levels, moral conduct, creative expressions, traditional ceremonies and community structure (Bailey et al. 2004; Mathieson & Wall 1990). Those are generally seen as negative impacts. Tourism can also have some impacts which are regarded as positive. It can prevent residents to move away from an area because of job creation, it can help to foster peace and it can create pride in a destination about cultural traditions (Bailey et al. 2004). Below is a more detailed description of some socio-cultural impacts.

Promotion of cross-cultural understanding
People often have a stereotypical view of other cultures, especially if they have never met anyone from that other culture. Meeting people from different cultures by means of tourism can reduce stereotypes and foster understanding of other cultures. Tourism can also be used as a force for

world peace, because people from different countries meet each other in the positive setting of tourism, instead of a possible negative setting of conflicting politics (Weaver & Lawton 2010).

Preservation of culture and heritage

Tourism can contribute to the preservation of ceremonies and tradition, protecting them from disappearing due to modernisation. If there would not be tourism demand for them, they might disappear completely. The same is true for the conservation of historical sites (Mathieson & Wall 1990; Weaver & Lawton 2010).

Promoting social wellbeing and stability

Because tourism generates revenue and employment, it contributes to the economic development and the social wellbeing and stability in a destination. Improvements in services and health standards implemented for tourists also benefit the local community. This impact can have the biggest effect in developing countries, since in developed countries those aspects are generally already better (Weaver & Lawton 2010).

Crowding

Tourism can affect local residents in several ways. The actual tourists can have an influence, by buying a service or just by being there. Many tourists will cause crowding and congestion (Mathieson & Wall 1990). In a survey by the Center on Ecotourism and Sustainable Development (2006) it became clear that cruise tourists in Belize had a negative effect on land based tourists due to crowding issues. For more than two thirds of the land based tourists, the cruise tourists had a negative impact on their experience and on the reputation of the nearest destination site. Overcrowding was said to be the main problem with cruise tourism, at tourist attractions and in the city. Belize used to have an image as being a peaceful and secluded nature destination, but this image is being threatened by the overcrowding caused by cruise tourism (Center on Ecotourism and Sustainable Development 2006).

Culture Clashes

Another influence of tourism is called the demonstration effect. It means that the hosts look up to the tourists and the things they have, and they want the same. This is more common in developing countries. Tourism is however not the only event contributing to the demonstration effect. Television and other media also play an important role in this. Also the effect can work both ways, so that locals can influence tourists as well as the other way around. Some very traditional locals can become even more conservative because of tourism, which is the opposite of the demonstration effect (Bailey *et al.* 2004; Mathieson & Wall 1990; Weaver & Lawton 2010). Other cultural clashes occur when tourists partly or completely ignore the customs and moral values of the host community. Also an impact of tourism is foreign ownership and employment. If the best jobs, e.g. management functions, get taken away by people from outside the area, this can invoke irritation amongst the local residents (Bailey *et al.* 2004; Mathieson & Wall 1990; Weaver & Lawton 2010).

Change of Identity and Values

A change of identity and values can occur in different ways, for example the emergence of well known brands, such as McDonald's, because these brands are more familiar to tourists (Bailey *et al.* 2004). Local rituals and traditions can be altered to make them more interesting for tourists, which is known as commodification. Also the local residents can make changes in the traditional crafts and arts which they make, to suit them more to the tourists, thereby losing the original crafts and arts (Bailey *et al.* 2004; Mathieson & Wall 1990; Weaver & Lawton 2010). Also the local residents might have to speak more and more the language of the tourists and might in the end lose their own language (Mathieson & Wall 1990).

Physical Influences causing Social Stress
It is possible that conflicts arise between tourists and local residents because of resources. For example if water is scarce, tourists might be able to get more of it, if they are able to pay more, so that the local residents have an even bigger shortage. Another way in which tourism causes stress amongst the locals is by means of vandalism, littering and stealing of cultural heritage. Also conflict can arise when land that was originally used for traditional land use is developed into tourist facilities (Bailey et al. 2004).

Prostitution and crime
Tourism may increase prostitution and crime. Tourists are often easier targets for crime than local residents, because tourists might carry around more money or valuable items, such as a camera. Also they might not know which parts of the destination are safe and which are not (Bailey et al. 2004; Mathieson & Wall 1990). Of course tourists are not always the victim, they also commit crimes, for example the participation in illegal prostitution. It is more complicated than that tourism directly causes higher crime rates. Development of tourism usually goes together with general development and modernisation of a destination. This general development can contribute as well to the increase in crime rate. Also, when more people move to the destination because of the development, both general and touristic, and the crime rate increase, it is possible that the crime rate per capita is still the same (Weaver & Lawton 2010).

2.2.3 Environmental impact

These days there is more and more concern for the environment. It is a popular trend for tourism businesses to become more environmentally friendly and ecotourism is on the rise. Following is an overview on the environmental impacts of tourism and more specifically cruise tourism.

Tourism can have some positive effects for the environment. It is preferential that a tourist destination is clean. If the destination is kept clean for touristic reasons, the local residents benefit from this as well. Also natural aspects such as forests, nice views and wildlife are important for tourism, so these have to be conserved. The local residents also benefit from keeping their natural surroundings. Tourists might also report when a natural area is disappearing for wrong reasons, thereby contributing to the preservation of it. And by seeing endangered natural sites, tourists can become more aware of the importance of protecting the environment (Weaver & Lawton 2010).

Examples of negative environmental impacts due to cruise tourism are harmful air emission, discharge of waste water and solid waste and the introduction of non-native species (Bailey et al. 2004).

There are international laws to prevent environmental damage from cruise ships, like SOLAS (the International Convention for the Safety of Life at Sea) and MARPOL (the International Convention for the Prevention of Pollution from Ships), but still a lot of raw sewage makes its way into the oceans every day. This sewage contains bacteria and viruses that are harmful to the environment, which makes the water unsafe for swimming and contaminates seafood. This can make people sick when they eat the contaminated seafood (Bailey et al. 2004).

The Organisation for Economic Cooperation and Development (Weaver & Lawton 2010)) formulated an environmental impact sequence. It uses a systems approach to model the environmental impacts of tourism and consists of four stages, which are stressor activities, environmental stresses, environmental responses and human responses. The stressor activities cause a certain stress on the environment, the environment responds to those stresses and then humans respond to the environmental responses. Both type of responses can be immediate or long term and range from direct to indirect. The human responses can become new stressor activities (Weaver & Lawton 2010).

Stressor activities can be divided into four categories, being 'permanent' environmental restructuring, generation of waste residuals, tourist activities and indirect and induced activities (Weaver & Lawton 2010).

'Permanent' environmental restructuring refers to alterations which are intended to be permanent and are made because of tourism. Examples are clearance of existing natural vegetation and levelling of the terrain. Environmental responses to clearance can be a reduction in biodiversity of native flora and fauna and an increase of exotic flora and fauna, which can be undesirable in the area. Levelling can cause responses such as soil erosion and landslides and in the long term it can cause flooding problems (Weaver & Lawton 2010).

Examples of waste residuals generated by tourism are blackwater (i.e. sewage), greywater (e.g. water from showers), garbage (organic and inorganic), atmospheric emissions and noise pollution. Environmental responses to blackwater can be amongst others water contamination and it can harm or kill marine life. Atmospheric emissions contribute to climate change (Weaver & Lawton 2010).

29

Some tourists stressor activities can be deliberate, such as littering, harassing wildlife or the destroying of vegetation by means of an off-road vehicle. Other stressor activities can be more unintentional, such as trail erosion or wildlife disruption due to high intensity of hiking or wildlife-viewing activities. Also tourists may introduce harmful pathogens into an area, which can wipe out part of the native fauna (Weaver & Lawton 2010).

As with revenue and employment, there are also indirect and induced impacts of tourism on the environment. Examples of indirect impacts are road improvements and airport expansions due to tourism. The building of houses for people who move to the area in order to work in the tourism industry is an induced impact (Weaver & Lawton 2010).

One way to calculate the environmental impacts of tourism is by using the ecological footprint (Weaver & Lawton 2010).

It is important to look at the impact on the natural environment as well as the built environment, especially cultural heritage sites and other important sites. Also the impact of cruise tourism can be divided in the impacts of the cruise ships and the impact of the passengers when they are on land. The biggest problem when the passengers go on land is the amount of them. Also it is important to consider whether cruise ships are worse for the environment compared to if all the passengers would go by their own cars or other alternative transportation. Then it should also be taken into account that they would need separate accommodation, while on a cruise this is included.

Tourism can contribute to the preservation and restoration of historical sites, for example because of entrance fees, sale of souvenirs and donation, as well as by general tourism revenues which are allocated to the preservation and restoration of historical sites (Weaver & Lawton 2010).

2.3 Residents attitudes to tourism

For tourism to be sustainable, it is important to meet the need of the tourists as well as the host regions. Not just in the present, but also with respect to the future. The management of the available resources should take into account both economic, socio-cultural and environmental sustainability, so that ecological processes and biological diversity, as well as cultural integrity and life support systems are maintained. Local initiatives are important in tourism development, so that local values can be taken into account and the local environment, community and culture are not harmed (Gursoy *et al.* 2009). It is important that the residents benefit from the tourism development and not suffer because of it. Therefore they should be able to participate in the management of the development (Andereck *et al.* 2005; Weaver & Lawton 2010). The acceptability of tourism by the local residents has a big effect on the success and sustainability of the tourism development. Therefore it is important for policy makers to understand the level of support from the residents towards the different developments in tourism (Gursoy *et al.* 2009). Then irritation can be avoided. If the attitudes of the residents are not taken into account, this can lead to opposition towards the tourism development, which can have great negative effects on the development (Gursoy & Rutherford 2004; Weaver & Lawton 2010). Residents can positively contribute to the planning management and marketing of tourism in a destination, by use of their knowledge of the area, for example about local history and cultural attractions (Weaver & Lawton 2010).

Doxey proposed a model to describe the general reaction of residents to tourism, known as the irritation index or irridex (Weaver & Lawton 2010). According to Doxey, people go through certain stages during the development of tourism: euphoria, apathy, annoyance, antagonism, resignation. Initially people are euphoric when just some tourists come to the destination. It is an interesting happening and it generates some extra

31

revenue. When more tourists come, residents start to take them for granted and the interactions become more commercial and commodified. This is the apathy stage. When more and more tourists come, residents go through stages of irritation and annoyance, before going into the antagonism stage. At this point the tourism approaches and exceeds the carrying capacities of the socio-cultural and natural environment. The residents realise that they have to adapt to the changed community. Some silently accept the situation, while others may choose to leave the area. The stages in Doxey's irridex are associated with different phases in Butlers resort cycle. During the exploration phase, there is pre-euphoria. During the involvement phase there is euphoria. During the development phase there is first apathy and later annoyance. During the consolidation and stagnation phases there is first antagonism and then resignation (Weaver & Lawton 2010).

Critiques to Doxey's irridex are that is takes the community as a homogeneous entity, while actually each resident might react differently to a certain phase in tourism development (Gibson & Bentley 2007). Residents reactions depend on factors as how much contact they have with tourists, how long they have lived in the destination, their socio-economic status and whether or not they work in the tourism industry (Weaver & Lawton 2010). Another important factor is how much revenue they derive from tourism (Gibson & Bentley 2007). Even just one person can have a mixed view of tourism. They may not like the tourism, because of its negative effects on the environment, but at the same time they might like tourism, because they can earn a lot of money from it. Or they might not like it personally, but appreciate the good effect it has on the community in general (Weaver & Lawton 2010).

Another critique to Doxey's irridex is that it assumes that the local community is passive, instead of actively taking measures to cope with the tourism in a positive way. Examples of measures that can be taken are zoning of frontstage and backstage, limiting the amount of visitors, limiting non-local ownership, education programs and improving of infrastructure (Weaver & Lawton 2010).

Below I describe some theories about residents attitudes, while comparing this to the findings of a survey done amongst residents in Falmouth, about cruise tourism (Gibson & Bentley 2007). This research was done to continue and develop the work of Liu and Var (1986), 'who stated that residents strongly agreed to the notion that tourism provides many economic and cultural benefits' (Gibson & Bentley 2007, p. 71). It is found that residents who work in tourism are generally more positive to tourists than those who do not work in tourism (Andereck et al. 2005). This was not the case in the Falmouth survey. Of the respondents, 46.6 percent had a job that had some relation to tourism. This was representative, because the tourism industry is the largest in the study area. However, because it is a small town, even those that have nothing to do with tourism because of their job, do encounter tourists in daily life. The response rate to the survey was high, indicating that the residents had a strong view of cruise tourism (Gibson & Bentley 2007).

Many residents, 40.5 percent, agree that the number of tourist attractions and facilities have increased due to cruise tourism (Gibson & Bentley 2007). According to Faulkner and Tideswell (1997), tourism has a positive effect on recreational, shopping and service facilities. Most residents in Falmouth were unsure about this, 41.7 percent, though when comparing agreements and disagreements, there were more agreements (Gibson & Bentley 2007). 'Jurowski, Uysal, and Williams (1997) argue that this could be as a result of residents not using the same resources as the tourists' (Gibson & Bentley 2007, p. 72). Faulkner and Tideswell (Faulkner & Tideswell 1997) found that tourism development has a positive effect on the quality of life in a community. Almost half of the residents of Falmouth were unsure whether tourism development had a positive effect on their lives, which could be because cruise tourism is a new industry in Falmouth and it is still growing. However, 84.6 percent of the respondents did not agree that the cruise tourists interfere with the way of life and 81 percent did not agree that the cruise tourists reduce their quality of life. Also cruise tourism has a strong effect on the pride of the Falmouth residents, since 61.9 percent agrees that cruise tourism has heightened their pride (Gibson & Bentley 2007).

Tourism is an important industry in Falmouth, illustrated by the high proportion of respondents that has a job related to tourism. Cruise tourism is an important part of the overall tourism. It has been identified that cruise tourism created employment and income opportunities to the residents of Falmouth (Gibson & Bentley 2007).

Several studies suggest that cruise tourists move around in packs when they are on the land and that the number of people in a destination increases considerably when a ship is in port, and that this concentration of tourists could lead to overcrowding and congestion (Jaakson 2004; Mathieson & Wall 1990). However, 50 percent of the residents in Falmouth disagreed with this and only 36.9 percent agreed. To put this into perspective, it is important to remember that the ships in Falmouth are relatively small, with generally around 184 passengers. Even though they arrive in Falmouth at the same time, most will go straight on a bus and go on a tour outside the city centre, so that the life of local residents is not as much affected as it could be if all the passengers would go into town (Gibson & Bentley 2007).

Most respondents, 84.5 percent, says that an increase in cruise tourism does not lead to an increase in crime levels (Gibson & Bentley 2007). Also the crime levels measured by the police had not increased (Gibson & Bentley 2007).

Since Falmouth has only been established as a home and destination port during the last five years, cruise tourism is still something new for the town. Therefore, when looking at Doxey's irridex, Falmouth residents are still euphoric about the cruise tourism. This is obvious from the reactions of the residents, who are excited about having cruise tourists in their town and visiting their hotels and attractions (Gibson & Bentley 2007).

Before the introduction of cruise tourism, Falmouth was in the stagnation phase of Butler's resort lifecycle. Due to the emergence of cruise tourism, the destination entered the rejuvenation phase instead of the decline phase (Gibson & Bentley 2007).

Understanding the impacts of tourism development is important, especially in small destinations. In many small destinations cruise tourism is a new industry. In the case of Falmouth, the positive social impacts seem to outweigh the negative social impacts, but cruise tourism is still new to the area, so during further development, the perception of the positive and negative impacts can still change (Gibson & Bentley 2007).

In Cyprus there has also been done a survey amongst residents. This was done in three different destinations. Two of them have had more tourism already, Ayia Napa and Paralimni, and one is still less developed, Kyrenia. According to the data, the residents in Kyrenia are more pro-tourism than the residents of the other two destinations. According to the Butler sequence, it is generally the case that destinations that have had less experience with tourism are still more positive about it than those that have had tourism for a longer period of time and where it has developed more. Butler hypothesises that when tourism grows in an area and there is more interaction between tourists and residents, the residents will start to be more resentful and hostile towards the tourists. However, in the survey on Cyprus, in all three locations respondents are more positive when interaction with tourists increases. More frequent contact with the tourists results in interactions being regarded as more positive. This would indicate that tourism in all three areas is still in the early stages of development and resentment has not yet emerged (Akis *et al.* 1996).

3. Methods

3.1 Choice of method

The starting point for the choice of method is the main research question, which in this study is:

How can a small destination develop cruise tourism in a sustainable way?

To answer this question, I choose to use a combination of primary and secondary data. The secondary data consist of articles, reports, etc for background information and theories. The primary data I collected by means of a case study in Skjolden, which is a small destination with a recent history of cruise tourism. The method of data collection used is semi-structured interviews. Also some interviews were taken in Olden and Flåm, which are also small destinations, but with a longer history of cruise tourism. The results from the interviews and the interpretations of them are compared to the general theory about the subject. I choose a qualitative method, because it allowed me to go more into depth about the specific case than would be possible with a quantitative method.

3.2 Data collection

3.2.1 Documentation

On the one hand secondary sources were used for constructing the theoretical part, which will help in answering the research questions and finally the main question. On the other hand the secondary data, mostly reports, are used to find more specific information, not general theories, e.g. reports about cruise tourism in Norway.

3.2.2 In-depth interviews

There are different methods for interviewing: structured, semi-structured and unstructured. In unstructured interviews the interviewer does not have a list of questions, but only a theme to talk about. Those kind of interviews are useful in a very early stage of exploring a subject, where the interviewer and the respondent together try to figure out what is important in the study (Ritchie *et al.* 2005). In semi-structured interviews the interviewer has a list of questions, but it is ok to change around the order of the questions and to elaborate more on certain questions, depending on what the respondents have to say (Hesse-Biber & Leavy 2011). Structured interviews have a set order of questions, which does not allow deviation. Very often this generates quantitative data (Ritchie *et al.* 2005). For this study, semi-structured interviews were used. There was not just a theme for the interviews, but a list of questions had already been constructed. However, it was useful to be able to deviate from the questions when the respondents had more to say and changing the order of the questions during the different interviews allowed for a better flow of the interview.

Interviews can be classified further. They can be quantitative or qualitative. Semi-structured interviews are generally qualitative in nature, as they are also in this study. Interviews can be taken with groups, pairs or individuals (Hoyle *et al.* 2002; Ritchie *et al.* 2005). I mostly interviewed individuals and some pairs, once because the interview was with the husband and wife together and one interview was with two respondents who knew each other and had proposed to do the interview together. This was convenient time wise and the two respondents could help each other out and built on each other's answers. Also interviews are classified by their purpose (Ritchie *et al.* 2005). The purpose of the interviews in this study was to achieve an understanding of the opinions, values and attitudes of the residents and to achieve an understanding of how cruise tourism affects a small destination.

38

3.2.3 Selection of respondents and taking the interviews

Interviews are also classified by the composition of the people who are involved in the interviews, for example an expert panel (Hoyle *et al.* 2002; Ritchie *et al.* 2005). In this study the respondents were certain residents of Skjolden and its direct surroundings, and some from Olden and Flåm. One of the criteria for selecting the respondents was that they have a connection with cruise tourism. Another criteria is that it was geographically possible to interview them. Since I did not have a car, I had to reach the respondents by public transport or by foot or they had to come to me, in which case we took the interview in a café or other public area. The other interviews were taken in people's homes or offices.

I had a contact person in Skjolden, who gave me a list of relevant people to interview. I contacted those people and asked them if they knew other people that were relevant. Also I asked if they knew relevant people in Olden and Flåm. I looked on the internet for more people with a connection to cruise tourism. Also during the interviews, some of the respondents tipped me about others, which I then also contacted and interviewed. This method of getting respondents is known as the snowball effect (Johannessen *et al.* 2010; Patton 2002). It turned out that not all the respondents had something to do with cruise tourism now, but most intended to in the future. One respondent did not have anything to do with cruise tourists directly, but it could influence the business indirectly. Everyone was willing to help, but some were not in the area at the time, and therefore I could not interview them.

Most of the respondents own a small tourism business and some own or are employees of a bigger tourism business. Some had already been receiving cruise tourists for a long time, some only recently and some had just started planning to receive cruise tourists. Some did not necessarily plan to receive cruise tourists, but if there would be interest from those tourists, they would look into it. Also some respondents were involved with tourism in another way, they were part of a tourism organisation or the cruise industry in their destination.

To help me through the interview, I had constructed an interview guide beforehand. I had two versions, one for the respondents that were part of a tourism business and one for the ones who were linked with tourism in a different way. The second one had some different questions for the different respondents, more specific to their job.

The interviews were held in English if that was acceptable to the respondent and otherwise in Norwegian. One was held in Dutch. The interviews took from 5 minutes to almost 2 hours, with most being between 15 minutes and an hour. All interviews were recorded, so I could transcribe and use them later.

Towards the end of the study I contacted one of the respondents again with some follow up questions.

3.3 Data analysis

Afterwards I transcribed the interviews. I left out the parts that were completely irrelevant to the study. Of the relevant part, I wrote some parts word for word and some I summarized, depending on the importance of the exact wording. In the transcribed text, I kept track of approximately in which minute something was said, so I could easily listen to the exact text again if needed.

During the whole process of collecting the data and transcribing it, I continued to collect and read more theoretical information, to help me to understand the subject better. Using this information, I divided the transcribed interviews into different parts, based on the same parts that I used in the theory, and thus based on the three research questions. This left me with for example a part of everything the respondents said about the economic effect of cruise tourism on the destination. I always wrote the name of the respondent who said it next to their text, so I could easily find it back in the recorded interview, for example to get the exact wording or more of the context.

Then I used the things that were said to write a text about it, also incorporating my interpretation and observation of the interviews and other information I collected during the interviews.

3.4 Validity and reliability

Validity is whether the data collected really reflects the problem that is being studied (Hoyle *et al.* 2002). External validity explains to what extent the findings of a study can be generalised and how representative they are for a population wider than the sample in the study. Important for this is how the sample is selected. Internal validity refers to how well the variables that are studied explain the concept or phenomena that is being studied. This can be difficult to achieve properly in tourism research, because it very often depends on people's behaviour and personal attitudes (Veal 2011).

Reliability is whether the data that is collected is correct. This could be found out by doing the same test again to see if it gives the same results (Hoyle *et al.* 2002). As with validity, perfect reliability is difficult to achieve in tourism research, because it is not based on controlled experiments, which can be easily replicated, but it deals with people's behaviour and attitudes. Even in the same situation, people do not always behave the same, so let alone if the situation has slightly changed (Veal 2011). Another problem with reliability for interviews could be that the respondents might answer things differently, because of the interviewer effect. Respondents might feel more comfortable with one interviewer than another, or the interviewer might have a different style of asking questions, which can all have an effect on the answers given by the respondents (Johannessen *et al.* 2010).

3.5 Ethical dilemma

An ethical dilemma with this kind of study is the anonymity of the respondents. Because the interviews were taken in a very small destination, there are only a limited number of certain businesses. There is for example only one lama farm in Skjolden, so if I would write about what the owner of the lama farm said, everyone would know who I mean. It is a little less obvious if I say what someone who holds animals said, because there are a few more respondents who hold animals, but still not a lot. It might not be important to all the respondents to stay anonymous, but some indicated that it is important for them, or at least with some of the questions. Therefore when I use the interviews in the results, I just mention that it was one of the respondents who said it. But if the thing that was said is more specific, people might still know who said it. However, I tried my best to disclose such information.

Also during the interviews, it is important that if one respondent has told you some personal information, that you do not tell this to any of the other respondents during the interviews. I have had some situations in which it would make sense to mention something that another respondent had said, but I realised that they might not want other people to know that, so I did not mention any of this to the other respondents.

4. Results

4.1 The role of Røysi, Luster municipality and the cruise companies

Already since 30 years ago, there was speculation in Skjolden about developing the cruise quay and attracting cruise tourism to Skjolden. From about 20 years ago, Luster municipality started talking about this more seriously, but they were never able to execute the plan, because there was not enough money available. Then, a number of years ago, Oddvar Røysi also came with the idea of developing cruise tourism in Skjolden. He saw it was a growing industry in other destinations and saw the potential for Skjolden. One of the reasons to choose Skjolden is that he is from the area himself and wanted to give something back. Apart from the cruise quay, he also bought the hotel and built apartments at the water side. Together they form Skjolden Resort. At the moment Røysi owns 51 percent of the cruise quay and Luster municipality owns the other 49 percent. Together they are a company called Skjolden Cruise Quay AS. In 2014 Røysi will buy out the municipality and own the quay completely. This was already agreed upon from the beginning. Skjolden Cruise Quay AS is payed a fee when ships dock in the harbour, but so far the company makes a loss, because costs are higher than the revenues. It is not clear why Røysi invested in the cruise quay when it makes a loss, but possibly it will start making a profit in a few years, because Skjolden is attracting more and more ships. Luster municipality did not invest in the quay because of direct revenue, but because of the infrastructural development and what it means for the development of tourism in the area. The profits of the increase in tourism and the development of Skjolden, making it a more attractive place to live in, outweigh the initial investment and losses associated to the quay.

Skjolden Cruise Quay AS makes the decision about how many cruise ships come to Skjolden. So far the intentions are to attract more cruise ships. There are not yet discussions of it becoming too much. When Luster municipality is no longer part of Skjolden Cruise Quay AS, they will not anymore be involved in this decision. They are however not afraid of losing control of the development of cruise tourism, partly because there is always politics involved in any development.

Cruise companies have of course also a big influence on the development of cruise tourism in Skjolden, because they are the customers. If the cruise companies do not want to come to Skjolden, and thus there is no demand for it, this will put a halt on the development. However, at the moment there do not seem to be any problems with getting the ships to Skjolden and the cruise industry is still growing.

4.2 Tourism development

4.2.1 Push and pull factors

Below are some push factors described that are relevant for cruise tourism. These push factors are influenced by the trends in this industry. The descriptions are based on what the respondents said and what is found in reports on cruise tourism. Since the push factors are not controllable by the destination, I only give a brief overview. Economic factors and demographic factors relate to that earlier only rich people could go on a cruise, but now also younger people and middle class families can do so. Social factors are that the image of cruise tourism gets better, so it is not anymore just for old people. Also people take shorter holidays, and thus also shorter cruises. Technological factors that increase the quantity of cruise tourism are that the ships are getting bigger, so more people can travel on it at the same time.

Also the newer ships are better for the environment than the old ships. This is important for some people.

More interesting are the pull factors, because they relate to the destination, and are therefore easier to influence by the destination. The destination in this study is Skjolden. Below the pull factors of Skjolden are described, based on information obtained in the interviews and information from reports about the area.

• Geographical proximity to markets

Skjolden does not lie in the best location when it comes to proximity to markets. The Sognefjord is the longest navigable fjord in the world, and Skjolden is located as far inland as large ships may go (Cruise Destination Skjolden - Sognefjord 2012). Therefore the cruise ships have to sail a long way before coming to Skjolden. This is something they take into account when choosing which destinations they visit.

• Accessibility to markets

The infrastructural accessibility of Skjolden is good. It has a large quay, which can accommodate even the biggest cruise ships. Also there will be an extra, mobile, quay in case there are two ships. Norway is a developed country, and Skjolden is a developed town, so there are no political problems for cruise tourism.

• Availability of attractions

Skjolden has a few bigger attractions and many smaller ones. Many attractions are natural ones, like the glacier, Sognefjellet, the waterfall, etc. The glacier used to have a visitor centre with a restaurant, souvenir shop and exhibition. This burned down, but is being replaced. There are also cultural attractions around Skjolden, like the Urnes stave church, which also has a visitor centre with restaurant and souvenir shop. There is another stave church and a normal, but very old, church in other towns around the destination. There is Skåri gård and Eide Besøksgård (visitor farm) in

Skjolden. There is the Witgenstein cabin. Also there is a juice museum in the area. There are people who have animals, in Skjolden there are deer and lama, and someone is thinking about having some small farm animals and horses. There are activities, such as kayaking and biking. And of course there are bus tours, just to enjoy the nature, for example up to Sognefjellet.

• Cultural links

Skjolden is located in a well developed western country. So far most cruise tourists come from other well developed western countries. Many Norwegians speak well English, which is nice for the tourists. A drawback with the similarity in culture is that tourists do not mainly come to Norway for experiencing a different culture. To use culture more as a pull factor, the host community could show more traditional Norwegian cultural happenings, even though they are not usually exhibited anymore.

• Availability of services

Bus trips are arranged for the cruise tourists and since it is a developed destination, practical services such as toilets are good. Also there is a tourist information centre and a café.

• Affordability

Norway is the second most expensive country of Europe, after Switzerland. But in the cruise everything is included, and the tourists do not have to buy anything in the destination. Cruises by itself are usually a bit more expensive than land based travel and cruises to Norway are more expensive than cruises e.g. in the Mediterranean or the Caribbean.

• Peace, stability and safety

Skjolden is a safe place, not prone to natural disasters and the drinking water is clean. The roads are not the best, but they are safe. The roads are more a problem if many people use them, in terms of congestion, but not a problem for safety.

- Positive market image

Much is done to market Skjolden as a cruise destination. Thereby it is also made use of the fact that Skjolden lies innermost in the longest fjord and at the foot of the highest mountains in Norway.

- Pro-tourism policies

In Flåm there is a project going to teach some residents more about the tourists and how to engage with them in a way that is positive for all. Such a method can be used in Skjolden as well, so that people are no longer annoyed by tourists who walk into their gardens, but can turn it into something positive.

4.2.2 Different stages in tourism development

Land based tourism in Skjolden was early in the development stage when cruise tourism came. According to Butler (1980), this stage is characterised by a tourism market area that is well defined and partly shaped by advertising. During this stage, there is a rapid decline in local involvement and control of the development. Some small local facilities are replaced by larger, more elaborate facilities which are provided by external organisations (Butler 1980). This is also seen in Skjolden, where the resort and the cruise quay are financed and partly managed from outside the area. It is a means to attract more tourists. The local residents did not have much choice, although some say that this is a reaction from a call for help with the quay from inside the community and that that is why Oddvar Røysi financed it. A certain loss of control is expressed by some residents, saying that even though they might not like cruise tourism, it is there, so they have to make the best of it.

Also more seasonal workers are needed and these are often not locals. Since 2012 the land agent, who takes care that the ship gets what it needs, is also not local anymore. Locally there are not enough busses, so they have to come from other areas as well.

Usually in the involvement stage it might be necessary to improve transport, Skjolden is a bit behind on this, so the roads can cause problems with the increased amount of visitors. One of the respondents said that they are doing things the wrong way around. First they built the resort and the quay and then look at how they can handle it.

During the development stage, the amount of visitors may exceed the number of residents, especially in small destinations (Butler 1980). Since Skjolden is a very small destination, this is definitely the case, especially since the largest cruise ships can carry more than 3000 passengers, which is ten times the amount of residents in Skjolden. When a destination enters the consolidation stage, the increase rate in visitors will decline, although the total number of visitors keeps growing (Butler 1980). Skjolden is still years away from the consolidation stage. The number of cruise ships visiting every year is rapidly growing. It has to be critically looked at whether the consolidation stage would far exceed the carrying capacity of Skjolden, and what alternatives there are.

The stagnation stage is characterised by reaching the peak number of visitors. Carrying capacity levels are reached or exceeded, both economic, socio-cultural and environmental. Although the image of the area will be well established, it will go out of fashion. Imported artificial facilities will supersede natural and genuine attractions (Butler 1980). I think Flåm never went into the stagnation stage. It did not go out of fashion and the big natural attraction has not been superseded by imported 'artificial' facilities, but just supplemented by it. The Flåmsbana will not easily go out of fashion, because it is one of the most beautiful train rides in the world. That is what keeps Flåm popular as a tourist destination. Tourism is the biggest form of revenue in Flåm, it is heavily reliant on tourism, which is already the case in the consolidation stage

(Butler 1980). During the consolidation stage, people that do not like the developments might leave the area (Weaver & Lawton 2010). I think this was the case in Flåm long ago, so people who live there now like the tourism industry or at least tolerate it.

Skjolden does not have one big attraction that will not go out of fashion, so they probably have to work harder on the management of the destination in order to keep the natural attractions and not get artificial attractions. Of course attractions such as the glacier and the stave church will not easily go out of fashion, but the question is whether this is enough for the large amount of visitors. To prevent the consolidation and stagnation stage, it is important to look at which alternative scenario can be applied to Skjolden. The best would probably be a combination of the supply-driven and the demand-driven scenario. Considering the demand-driven scenario, Skjolden has to figure out what their threshold is, how they can increase it and how much. Then, taking into consideration the threshold, they have to use the supply-driven scenario to make sure the threshold is not exceeded.

There are a number of factors that can influence the destination cycle, in each case it can be stimulants or depressants:
• internal-intentional
How Skjolden copes with the growing cruise industry is something internal and intentional. They can take actions that are stimulants or depressants. A depressant would be to limit the number of cruise ship that can come on a day, during a week or in total during the season. Of course this would limit the revenue of the harbour. Therefore instead of just limiting the amount of ships that can come to the destination, they can increase the price for having the ship in the harbour. This will lead to less ships coming to the destination, but with possibly the same amount of revenue for the harbour. The same can be done with prices of other services and attractions. A stimulant could be

improving the road and making attractions more available to tourists, for example by reducing prices, and marketing and innovation.

• external-unintentional

In the summer of 2011 there was a lot of rain in Skjolden, this is external and unintentional. When the weather is bad, more cruise tourists stay on the ship, so this is a depressant. One respondent said that 'Due to last year's bad weather, many people did not come off the boats, just went on walks.' Another respondent said that with bad weather, less people come to visit his animals. Also climate change can have a depressing impact. Due to climate change, the glacier melts, resulting in the deterioration or eventually disappearance of an attraction. An external unintentional stimulant can be when another destination cannot receive a ship and it therefore comes to Skjolden. This can be because the other destination has reached its capacity or because something happened so that the ship cannot go there. One of the respondents said that some ships come to Skjolden, because Flåm has reached its capacity.

• internal-unintentional

One respondent mentioned that the apartments of the resort are higher than they were supposed to be according to the plans beforehand. This is an internal unintentional factor which could be a depressant to residents who expected them to be less high. On the tourists this will however have less effect, since they did not know about the plans, so they only experience the apartments as they are now.

• external-intentional actions

The investment of Oddvar Røysi in the resort and the cruise quay was external and intentional and it is a stimulant. Also the preservation of attractions like the stave church are financed from externally and are stimulants. The organisation of the cruise industry and domination of the cruise market by three big companies (Bailey *et al.* 2004; World Tourism Organization 2010) is external, intentional and can be either a stimulant or a depressant. Those three big companies are Carnival, Royal Caribbean Cruises and Star Cruises (Page 2011).

4.2.3 Differences between cruise tourism and land based tourism

As described earlier, tourism consists of four parts; activities, accommodation, food and transport (Kamfjord 2003). From the interviews it is clear that in cruise tourism most of the aspects of tourism takes place on the ship. The tourists sleep on the ship and the ship is their transport from destination to destination. However, when they are at a destination, they need local transport to get around. Many cruise tourists go on a bus tour around the area, to view the beautiful nature and to visit attractions that are further away. Since the quay is a fair walk away from the town centre, it is also useful to have some transportation between the quay and the town centre. While in port, some passengers might choose to stay on the ship and continue enjoying the activities on board, but most will visit activities and attractions on land.

All food is included on the ship. This makes it more difficult to arrange whole day tours, as one respondent stated: 'All the food is included. Many go back for lunch if they can. Relax on the boat. Those do not go on trips. Also many trips come back for lunch. There are different combinations. Some come in the morning and eat here, some go back for lunch and then do a bus tour.' and 'There haven't been many tours with lunch included, short ones are easier to sell, shorter and cheaper.'

The cruise companies try to get the tours as cheap as possible, so they can make the most money of it. Including lunch on a tour would make it more expensive. It would be interesting to include a traditional Norwegian lunch, but food in Norway is expensive. The food on the ship is cheaper. It is more feasible to have a coffee and cake break included on the tours.

There has also been organised a market with local food products on days that there were cruise ships. This did not work out as planned. Most cruise tourists only came to taste some products, but did not buy anything. Also in the local food shop, cruise tourists are not big customers. It depends a bit on where they come from. Americans for example tend to buy more than Germans. They would not generally buy food, but mostly postcards and stamps and some body lotion or soap.

When talking to accommodation owners, there is a mixed view of the impact of cruise tourism. One has nothing to do with it. It is possible that cruise tourism attracts more land based tourists to Skjolden, because of curiosity, but it is also possible that the mass tourism of cruises scares away land based tourists. If it attracts more land based tourists, this will benefit accommodations, but if it scares them away, this will have a negative effect on accommodations. In Skjolden the situation is somewhat special, because the resort is built along with the cruise quay, from the same investments. The resort consists of the hotel, which was already there, and apartments along the water. People involved in the resort are positive that there will be more land based tourism in Skjolden and that the cruise tourism can help achieving this.

When cruise ships come to a destination, there are three important roles to be filled. The harbour master makes sure the ship can dock, and welcomes the cruise tourists, the agents provide the ship if they need anything and the land operator organises tours.

Up to 2011, the land operator function was done by Reisemål Sogndal og Luster. Since 2012 this has been taken over by Geiranger Cruise Handling, a company that is owned mainly by International Travel Group located in Bergen and involved in tourism in several other parts of Norway. This is an example of typical development in most industries due to the economics of scale (Weng & Wang 2004). However, the harbour master is local, not from Skjolden, but he lives not far from Gaupne.

4.3 Impacts of tourism development

Below I describe the impacts of cruise tourism on Skjolden, based on interviews with the local residents and my interpretations. Different people say different things about cruise tourism, because they have different views and opinions about it, but they also contradict each other on issues that are not opinions, but 'facts'. Some say that most residents like cruise tourism, while others say that most residents don't like it. Of course this cannot both be true. I will describe both sides of such contradictions.

4.3.1 Economic impact

Revenue / More money from land based tourists compared to cruise tourists

When talking about direct revenue, and especially that there is less direct revenue in cruise tourism than in land based tourism, there is general agreement. Respondents say that cruise tourists sleep and eat on board the cruise ship and therefore the destination does not earn from this. Some tours have lunch included or a coffee and cake stop, so a little money can be earned on food, but most say that many tourists do not want a tour with lunch included, but prefer a half day tour, so that they can have lunch on the ship, because it is included.

However, there is money in cruise tourism. One respondent said that: 'You often read there is no money in cruise, but then you read Flåm missed out on a ship and missed a million. This Italian boat that sunk should have come to Norway and they lose money because of it.' How much of this money benefits the destination, depends on what the residents do to receive the money. Some respondents argue that some people say that they do not earn money from cruise tourism, but this is logical if they have nothing to offer. You have to offer a product or service to the cruise tourists, in order to be able to earn money from them.

Even though cruise tourists spend less money per person, they may still leave a lot of money behind in a destination, simply because they are many. Also cruise tourism is a form of marketing. Cruise tourists might decide to come back as land based tourists or even again as a cruise tourist, and they might tell their family and friends about how much they liked Skjolden, so that some of the people they told about it may travel there.

A problem with cruise tourism is that the cruise companies want as low prices as possible for the activities during tours. The service providers themselves get a small part of the income, and the rest goes to the land operator and the cruise company. One of the respondents explained that this way cruise tourists pay a lot more than land based tourists, while the service providers do not benefit from that. They can only offer a minimum for the money they get. For example, when cruise tourists visit a glacier, they will only quickly look at the glacier. They don't go on the glacier, which is of course also for a great part because they do not have time for it, because they only want a half day tour.

So far in Skjolden cruise tourism is an extra income for some residents who have something to offer. No one has cruise tourism as their only source of income, and this would not yet be possible, because so far there have only been cruise ships on a few days each summer. Maybe in a few years time, when more cruise ships come, it would be possible for some people to have cruise tourism as their main source of income, as is already the case in Olden.

Job opportunities

Every form of tourism creates jobs, so also cruise tourism. The problem with cruise tourism is that initially there are only ships in Skjolden a few days each summer, so there is only more work for a few days and it is seasonal. It is important to have local guides, because they know the area.

Entrepreneurial activity, economic structure and infrastructure

One of the respondents said that he extended his business to Skjolden, before anyone else would start offering the same. Since there is cruise tourism, he wants to make the best out of it. The improvement of part of the road and the new tunnel close to Skjolden, was not a reaction to the increase in cruise tourists, but would be done anyways. The infrastructure is still not good enough to receive all the land based tourists and cruise tourists who come to the area during summer. One respondent said that concerning the cruise tourism, 'people in Skjolden are excited that something is happening'. In contrast to neighbouring towns, Skjolden does not experience people moving away and schools being put down, but an increase in job opportunities.

Opportunity costs

It could become a problem that the resources that are used for cruise tourism cannot be used for land based tourism, so that land based tourists are affected that way. It is not yet the case that land is used for tourism instead of farming. If at all, it is used for both.

Overdependence on tourism

There are no problems with overdependence on cruise tourism. For the moment it is rapidly growing. But even without the cruise tourism, there would still be the land based tourism. For most residents, if they do something with cruise tourism, it is only a small part of their business. However, they should be careful if they start directing just to cruise tourists. Although when looking at other destinations, there are no indications that cruise tourism will diminish.

Inflation and land values

There are not yet problems with getting enough land for tourism. For building the resort, someone had to sell that piece of land, but that was no problem, because they were not using it anyways, and by selling it, they made some money from it. It is not likely that the prices in the shop will increase because of tourists who have more money to spend than locals. Prices in Norway are already very high, so this might even cause tourists to buy less.

4.3.2 Social and cultural impacts

Since Skjolden is a small place, not just the residents that are employed in tourism will have encounters with the cruise tourists. Most of the residents will encounter cruise tourists on days that there is a ship in port. Some of the respondents mentioned that sometimes cruise tourists walk into residents gardens and look through the windows of their houses. Something has to be done to prevent this, because otherwise it will only get worse when more ships come. There is only one small food shop in Skjolden, which means that both residents and cruise tourists use the same services. This is also true for the café and other services. One of the respondents noticed that on days that there are cruise tourists, some of the residents went to a neighbouring town for their shopping, to avoid the crowdedness in the small shop in Skjolden. On the other side, residents do not just avoid contact, they also seek it. Often when a ship comes into the harbour, the band plays to welcome the tourists, and other residents might go to the café to look at and enjoy the happenings at the harbour.

Culturally and economically cruise tourists are usually to a great extend alike to the residents. Norway is a wealthy country and that does not vary much between the big cities and more rural areas. Most cruise tourists are also wealthy, though it becomes more and more accessible to average people as well. In both cases they are much alike the residents of Skjolden. Since most cruise tourists come from western countries, there is not a big cultural difference. There may be small cultural differences, like the time at which people eat dinner. This can be taken into account when planning tours.

Promotion of cross-cultural understanding is not a big issue here, because there is not much cultural difference between the residents and the cruise tourists. Preservation of culture and heritage is going on in Skjolden, for example at Skåri gård and the Witgenstein cabin, but this is not because of cruise tourism. At most it is partly because of tourism in general. Cruise tourism is not a big promoter for social wellbeing and stability. It does not lead to improvement of services like health care etc, because cruise tourists are only in the destination during the day and have their own services on board the ship.

Crowding

All respondents say it is it important that Skjolden does not get too many cruise ships. What is too many differs a bit per person. Some say one a day is ok, but not more. Some rather have less, for example two per week. As long as it does not become too many ships, people do not think there will be a problem with crowding. When saying that they do not want too many ships, many people refer to Flåm and some also to Geiranger. They say it is an industry there, it is too crowded and people have to wait in line too much. Some respondents have talked to cruise tourists who said that they should not destroy the quiet, nice place. It should not become so commercial, because then the kindness and quietness will disappear.

It is important to split up the cruise tourists, so that there are not too many at the same time in the same place. Flåm has one big attraction and some smaller ones. Skjolden has mainly many small attractions, some can only take around 10 people. It is a logistic challenge to spread the people over all those attractions.

Culture Clashes

In Skjolden there are no problems with the demonstration effect, because it is a developed area. There might however arise a problem with management jobs taken up from outside the area. Already the land agent job is now done from another town.

Change of Identity and Values

In Skjolden they are trying to sell genuine souvenirs, not the cheap kind that is made on the other side of the world. Even though residents have to speak English and other languages to the cruise tourists, they will not lose their original language, because the cruise tourists are there for a limited amount of time.

Skjolden does not experience major physical Influences causing social stress or an increase in prostitution and crime due to cruise tourism.

4.3.3 Environmental impact

Respondents are not very concerned for the environment when it comes to cruise tourism. The only critique is that it would be better if ships while at port were connected to electric supply from land, so they do not need to have their engines running all day. Also the older ships are worse for the environment, so it is better if they do not come. The newer ships are improving, so in the future there should not be a problem. Also it would be worse if all cruise tourists would come with their own car or by plane.

There are no problems for the protected areas, because the cruise tourists hardly come into them. Apart from that there is no difference between the cruise tourists and the land based tourists.

4.4 Residents attitudes to tourism

The respondents have a mixed view about cruise tourism. Also when asked what others think about it, they give very different answers. One respondent that is positive, because something is happening, says that he heard very little complains. Of course there are always people that do not want change, but the respondent thinks that this change and development is good for Skjolden.

Another respondent has a mixed view. On the one hand, he does not like cruise tourism. He is afraid for the environment and that there will be mass tourism. On the other hand, the extra tourism is good for his business. Since the cruise tourism is there anyways, he might as well make the most of it. If it does not become too large scale, it does not have to be a problem.

Yet another respondent also has a mixed view, but leans towards being positive. She says that the residents like that something is happening and that at least 90 percent is positive, as long as it does not become too large scale.

One respondent tells that in neighbouring towns, schools are closing down and people are moving away. In Skjolden this is the opposite. It is good that cruise tourism generates jobs, although it is mostly in summer. It would be better to have jobs more year round.

Another respondent says it is a bit early to know whether cruise tourism is a good development for Skjolden. It could be positive for the people that have something to offer, but it depends on how much money cruise tourists leave behind. She heard that people are negative, because there is less money in cruise tourism, amongst other things because they have lunch onboard the ship. But time will tell whether cruise tourism is a good development or not.

The respondents that are positive themselves, generally say that others are also positive.

When looking at Doxey's irridex, most of the respondents are still euphoric towards cruise tourists. Land based tourism is already more established, and therefore the respondents are more in the apathy stage towards them. Cruise tourism is new, and the respondents are curious how it will develop and whether they can benefit from it. However, some respondents are also leaning towards irritation and annoyance. Whether they will go into these stages depends on how the cruise tourism develops further, how many ships will come to Skjolden, whether the respondents can actually benefit from it and what other positive and negative effects it will have.

5. Discussion

Something very important for the sustainable development of a destination is to know who has the influence to make a change. In the case of cruise tourism in Skjolden, there are three main entities with a large influence. One of them is Oddvar Røysi. He can influence the development, because he has the money to do so. If he had not invested in the cruise quay and no one else had either, then the cruise quay could not have been built. Also the three main cruise companies have a lot of power. Thirdly, Geiranger Cruise Handling is a big player, as it is part of an even bigger cruise handling service located in Bergen.

The small business owners can only react to the changes made by the three main entities. As one of the respondents mentioned, the cruise tourism is there now, so he could better make the best out of it. When it comes to sustainable development, small businesses can decide to operate their own business in a sustainable way, but they cannot influence the destination as a whole. It is Skjolden Cruise Quay AS who makes the final decision about how many ships come to Skjolden. Geiranger Cruise Handling organises where the trips on land are going. If a small business wants to receive cruise tourists, they can talk about this to Geiranger Cruise Handling, which has the final say in the matter, together with the cruise companies, because they are the ones that decide what kind of trips they want to offer their guests.

Therefore, even once the destination knows about the impacts of cruise tourism and how to influence the impacts, it is still important to find out who can influence them and contact those people. The question is also what the role of the municipality is in the matter and how much influence they have and to what extent they can work together with the three main entities. Also politics are in play, so that the three main entities mentioned above will not have complete power and the destination, including its residents, still remain a level of control over the development.

5.1 Shortcomings of this study

One of the main shortcomings of this study is that there has not been enough focus on those three big influences. In the beginning it was not yet clear that those three entities would play such an important role in the development of Skjolden and therefore they have not been interviewed. Also in the interviews that were taken, they were not one of the focus points and therefore only occasionally something was mentioned about some of them. The same is true for the role of the municipality of Skjolden. Towards the final stages of this study, I tried to find out a bit more about this issue by calling one of the respondents for some follow up questions. That way I managed to get some more information on the role of Røysi, the municipality and the cruise companies in the development of cruise tourism in Skjolden. I then incorporated this in the results.

5.2 Choice of study area

The problem with Skjolden as a case is that the cruise quay was built at the same time as the resort was expanded. This was not a reaction to more tourism because of the cruise tourism, but it was done at the same time, by the same person. Therefore increase in jobs and income from tourism cannot just be accounted to cruise tourism.

5.3 Validity and reliability of the data

5.3.1 Validity

I did almost only ask people who are involved with cruise tourism, but some said that they only like it, because they can earn from it, indicating that they would not like it if they could not earn from it. Nevertheless it would be interesting to find out about the attitudes of the people who have nothing to do with cruise tourism or those who cannot earn from it.

With case studies, it is always difficult to generalise the findings. That is not any different in this study. The findings can help to increase the knowledge of how cruise tourism affects a small destination, but cannot be generalised by itself. Many such case studies are needed, in different destinations, to be able to form a generalisation. Also in this study not all the impacts mentioned by the respondents can be accounted to cruise tourism, since the resort and therefore the land based tourism was developed at the same time.

5.3.2 Reliability

Perfect reliability is difficult to obtain in qualitative research. What the respondents have told me could have been somewhat different if I would have talked to them on a different day. However, the respondents seemed at ease during the interviews and willing to tell what they know and their point of view. They did not seem to be holding back important issues, although one can never be sure about such things. The atmosphere during the interviews was good and I was interested in what the respondents told me, encouraging them to tell more.

Reliability also depends on my interpretation of the results. It is important that I have extensive knowledge about the topic in order to interpret the results properly. Therefore I started reading about relevant theories before the interviews, to know what kind of questions I should ask. During the entire process of interviews and writing the master thesis, I kept reading more relevant theories, and would rethink my interpretation of the results when necessary.

6. Conclusion

6.1 Cruise tourism development in a small destination

In order to develop tourism in a destination, several factors are important to know and to take into account. First of all it is important to know why tourists come to the destination at all. Push factors describe why people go on holidays, but this is not something that can be influenced by the managers of a destination. For them, it is more important to look at the pull factors of their destination, to find out why tourists come to their destination instead of going somewhere else. Not all pull factors can be influenced, but they can still be taken into account, for example in the marketing of the destination. Some pull factors, like natural attractions, can be maintained and improved in ways such as making paths for easier accessibility. Also new attractions can be created. Thereby is has to be kept in mind that different kind of attractions attract different kind of tourists.

For a sustainable tourism development it is important to manage the development from the beginning, so as to not let it get out of hand or taken over by external organisations. It is important to find out what factors can be influenced and which cannot be influences and how to deal with the different factors in the best way possible. Also it is useful to have a long term vision of how the destination should be developed, taking into account whether it is desirable to receive mass tourism or small scale tourism, what type of tourism, how the destination and its residents will benefit from it and so on.

When a destination is developing cruise tourism, it is important to keep in mind that certain processes are different for cruise tourism than for land based tourism. Cruise tourism is not often overnight tourism, the tourists get most of what they need on board the ship, they come on shore for a certain amount of time during the day. One ship can have more than 3000 passengers and cruise ships are still being built bigger. Many passengers will go on half day trips and some will go on day trips. Many busses and guides are needed during days of ship calls, while on days that there is no ship, none of this is needed and the destination is left with only land based tourists. This makes the biggest difference in small destinations.

To develop a destination in a sustainable way it is essential to know what the impacts of the development are. If one does not know the impacts, one cannot plan for sustainable development. Although impacts are usually divided into economical, socio-cultural and environmental, there is much overlap. Also they should be all equally important, although some people find the one impact more important while others find another one more important. Therefore it is important that all residents are involved in the development of the destination. On average the development should be more positive than negative, for most possible residents. Otherwise their might be resistance from the residents, which can have disastrous effects on the development.

6.2 Important impacts of cruise tourism

Some residents of a developing destination complain that they do not earn any money from tourism, but of course in order to benefit from it, they have to have something to offer. Ways of earning money from cruise tourism is by opening a business which offers activities or services. Cruise tourists are mostly interested in activities, because most of the services are provided on board the ship. Other jobs that are created because of cruise tourism are guiding jobs, driving buses and selling souvenirs. There are also some management jobs in cruise tourism, like organising the tours that can be taken on land and management of ships arriving in the harbour. It is important that local people get those jobs, both for economic and social reasons. Also that way, the destination has most control over the development. There are also indirect jobs related to increased cruise tourism. One example is that when traffic increases, the roads need improving, and people are needed to do the work on the roads. A problem with jobs related to cruise tourism is that they are highly seasonal, except for some of the planning jobs and some indirect jobs.

One of the major social impacts of cruise tourism is crowding and congestion. Especially in small destinations, the large number of cruise tourists coming on shore, have a tremendous impact. So far in Skjolden the number of tourists has not yet been seen as a problem, but many respondents are afraid that if more and more ships come to Skjolden, it will become more like Flåm, where it is very crowded when there are cruise ships in port, and people have to wait in line for the attractions. So far it is not yet a problem in Skjolden, because the people that come on shore are mostly separated over different tours and are therefore spread out over the area. This is however something that has to be managed properly with increasing visitor numbers. It has to be found out how the tourists can be spread out optimally and what other measures can be taken to prevent crowding, so to what extent the carrying capacity can be extended. If no more measures can be taken, Skjolden should consider refraining from letting more cruise tourists come at the same time, to prevent exceeding of the carrying capacity.

Since most cruise tourists come from western countries, as Norway is too, the differences in cultures will be small and not cause to many problems.

When it comes to environmental impacts, it is important to find out about the carrying capacities of the area and make sure that those are not exceeded. Also it could be useful to only allow ships in Skjolden, who operate a certain level of environmental friendliness, to contribute to the demand for the development of more environmentally friendly ships. This could be a good way of selecting which ships can come and which cannot, when carrying capacities, both environmental as economic and socio-cultural, are approached.

6.3 Suggestions for further research

As said in the discussion, it is important to look at who can influence the development and impacts of cruise tourism. In the case of Skjolden the most influential actors are large investors like Oddvar Røysi, the largest cruise companies, and tour operators like Geiranger Cruise Handling. Also it is important to know what the role of Luster municipality is and how politicians and the administration can work together with the three important groups of players just mentioned. Unfortunately this was not a main point of focus from the beginning of this research and therefore this remains unclear. It would be useful to further investigate this is future studies.

7. References

AKIS, S., PERISTIANIS, N. & WARNER, J. 1996. Residents' attitudes to tourism development: the case of Cyprus. *Tourism Management* 17:481-494.

ANDERECK, K. L., VALENTINE, K. M., KNOPF, R. C. & VOGT, C. A. 2005. Residents' perceptions of community tourism impacts. *Annals of Tourism Research* 32:1056-1076.

ANDERSEN, C. & ELLINGSEN, W. 2003. Reiselivsnæringer og turistkonsum i Hordaland. Samfunns- og Næringslivskorskning AS, Bergen.

BAILEY, K. S., MANSOUR, S. E., SILUE, R. & SINGLETON, D. 2004. Sustainable Tourism and the Cruise Line Industry. *Kenan-Flagler Business School*. University of North Carolina, Chapel Hill.

BUTLER, R. W. 1980. The Concept of a Tourist Area Cycle of Evolution: Implications for Management of Resources. *Canadian Geographer* 24.

CENTER ON ECOTOURISM AND SUSTAINABLE DEVELOPMENT. 2006. Cruise Tourism in Belize: Perceptions of Economic, Social & Environmental Impact.

CRUISE DESTINATION SKJOLDEN - SOGNEFJORD. 2012. Skjolden, Sognefjord, In the Heart of Norway.

CRUISE NORWAY. 2011. Markedsplan 2012. Cruise Norway.

DWYER, L. & FORSYTH, P. 1998. Economic Significance of Cruise Tourism. *Annals of Tounsm Research* 25:393-415.

FAULKNER, B. & TIDESWELL, C. 1997. A framework for monitoring community impacts of tourism. *Journal of Sustainable Tourism* 5:3-28.

G.P. WILD (INTERNATIONAL) LIMITED & BUSINESS RESEARCH & ECONOMIC ADVISORS. 2011. The Cruise Industry, a Leader in Europe's Economic Recovery. *Contribution of Cruise Tourism to the Economies of Europe*. European Cruise Council.

GIBSON, P. & BENTLEY, M. 2007. A Study of Impacts—Cruise Tourism and the South West of England. *Journal of Travel & Tourism Marketing* 20:63-77.

GURSOY, D., CHI, C. G. & DYER, P. 2009. Locals' Attitudes toward Mass and Alternative Tourism: The Case of Sunshine Coast, Australia. *Journal of Travel Research* 49:381-394.

GURSOY, D. & RUTHERFORD, D. G. 2004. Host attitudes toward tourism. *Annals of Tourism Research* 31:495-516.

HANDELSDEPARTEMENTET, N.-O. 2012. Destinasjon Norge, Nasjonal strategi for reiselivsnæringen.

HESSE-BIBER, S. N. & LEAVY, P. 2011. *The practice of qualitative research* (Second edition edition). SAGE Publications, Inc.

HOYLE, R. H., HARRIS, M. J. & JUDD, C. M. 2002. *Research Methods in Social Relations* (Seventh edition edition). Wadsworth.

JAAKSON, R. 2004. Beyond the Tourist Bubble? *Annals of Tourism Research* 31:44-60.

JOHANNESSEN, A., TUFTE, P. A. & CHRISTOFFERSEN, L. 2010. *Introduksjon til samfunnsvitenskapelig metode* (4. utgave edition). Abstrakt forlag AS.

KAMFJORD, G. 2003. *Reiselivsproduktet* (Third edition). WS Bookwell, Finland.

LIU, J. C. & VAR, T. 1986. Resident attitudes toward tourism impacts in Hawaii. *Annals of Tourism Research* 13:193-214.

MATHIESON, A. & WALL, G. 1990. *Tourism: economic, physical and social impacts*. Longman Scientific & Technical, Essex.

NHO REISELIV. 2010. Samarbeid - lønnsomhet - bærekraft. *cruise og landbasert reiseliv*.

PAGE, S. J. 2011. *Tourism Management, An Introduction* (Fourth edition edition). Elsevier Ltd.

PATTON, M. Q. 2002. *Qualitative Research & Evaluation Methods* (Third edition edition). Sage Publications, Inc.

RITCHIE, B. W., BURNS, P. & PALMER, C. 2005. *Tourism research methods: Integrating theory with practice*. CABI publishing.

VEAL, A. J. 2011. *Research methods for leisure & tourism, a practical guide* (Fourth edition edition). Pearson Education Limited.

WEAVER, D. B. & LAWTON, L. 2010. *Tourism Management* (Fourth edition). John Wiley & Sons Australia, Ltd, Milton.

WENG, C.-C. & WANG, K.-L. 2004. Scale and scope economies of international tourist hotels in Taiwan. *Tourism Management* 25:761-769.

WORLD TOURISM ORGANIZATION. 2010. Cruise Tourism, Current Situation and Trends. World Tourism Organization, Madrid.

CPSIA information can be obtained at www.ICGtesting.com
Printed in the USA
LVOW08s1716210314

378421LV00003B/651/P